I0407891

Beautiful Mandalas

Copyright: Published in the United States by Eric Tincher
Published January 2017
ISBN-13: 978-1542614184
ISBN-10: 154261418X

Thank you

www.ingramcontent.com/pod-product-compliance
Lightning Source LLC
Chambersburg PA
CBHW081554280526
45788CB00011B/3472